Treasury of
Italian Love

More *Treasury of Love*

Treasury of Arabic Love
Treasury of Finnish Love
Treasury of French Love
Treasury of German Love
Treasury of Hungarian Love
Treasury of Jewish Love
Treasury of Polish Love
Treasury of Roman Love
Treasury of Russian Love
Treasury of Spanish Love
Treasury of Ukrainian Love

Each collection also available as an Audio Book

HIPPOCRENE BOOKS
171 Madison Avenue
New York, NY 10016

A Treasury of Italian Love

Poems, Quotations & Proverbs

In Italian and English

Edited and translated by
Richard A. Branyon

HIPPOCRENE BOOKS
New York

Contents

Italian Love Poems

Italian Love Quotations and Proverbs
follow page 87

Italian Love Poems

Jacopo da Lentini (c. 1180-1250)

Madonna e il paradiso

Io m'aggio posto in core a Dio servire
  Com' io potesse gire in Paradiso,
  Al santo loco, ch'aggio audito dire,
  O' si mantien sallazzo, gioco e riso.
Sanza Madonna non vi vorría gire,
  Quella ch' ha bionda testa e chiaro viso,
  Che sanza lei non potería gaudire,
  Istando da la mia donna diviso.
Ma non lo dico a tale intendimento
  Perch' io peccato ci volesse fare;
  Se non veder lo suo bel portamento,
E lo bel viso e 'l morbido sguardare:
  Chè 'l mi terría in gran consolamento
  Veggendo la mia donna in gioia stare.

Jacopo da Lentini

Of His Lady in Heaven

I have it in my heart to serve God so
  That into Paradise I shall repair,
  The holy place through the which everywhere
  I have heard say that joy and solace flow.
Without my lady I were loath to go,—
  She who has the bright face and the bright hair;
  Because if she were absent, I being there,
  My pleasure would be less than nought, I know.
Look you, I say not this to such intent
  As that I there would deal in any sin:
  I only would behold her gracious mien,
And beautiful soft eyes, and lovely face,
  That so it should be my complete content
  To see my lady joyful in her place.

          D.G. Rossetti

Anonymous (c. 1200)

Strambotti Siciliani

Non mi mandar messaggi, ché son falsi;
Non mi mandar messaggi, ché son rei.
Messaggio sieno gli occhi quando gli alsi,
Messaggio sieno gli occhi tuoi a' miei.
Riguardami le labbra mie rosse,
Ch' aggio marito che non le conosce.

Più che lo mele hai dolce la parola,
Saggia e onesta, nobile e insegnata,
Hai le bellezze della Camiola,
Isotta la bioanda e Morgana la fata.
Se Bianchifiori ci fossi ancora,
Delle bellezze la giunta è passata.
Sotto le ciglia porti cinque cuose:
Amore e foco e fiamma e giglio e rose.

Anonymous

Sicilian Love Songs

Send no messages, for they are lies;
Send no messages, for they are sin;
No message save the uplifting of the eyes;
No message save your glance that comes to win
The knowledge of my lips how red they be.
Ah, men are bats, fair hues no husbands see!

     Cecil C. Palmer

More than honey the words you speak are sweet,
Honest and wise, nobly and wittily said,
Yours are the beauties of Camiola complete,
Of Iseult the blonde and Morgana the fairy maid.
If Blanchefleur should be added to the group,
Your loveliness would tower above each head.
Beneath your brows five beautiful things repose:
Love and a fire and flame, the lily, the rose.

     L.R. Lind

Pier della Vigna (c. 1200-1249)

Amore (1-32)

Amore, in cui disio ed ò speranza,
di voi, bella, m'à dato guiderone;
guardomi infin che vegna la speranza,
pur aspetando bon tempo e stagione:
Com'om ch'è in mare ed à spene di gire,
quando vede lo tempo ed ello spanna,
e giamai la speranza no lo 'nganna:
così faccio, Madonna, in voi venire.

Or potess'eo venire a voi, amorosa,
come larone ascoso e non paresse!
be 'l mi teria in gioia aventurosa,
se l'amor tanto bene mi faciesse.
Sì bel parlante, donna, con voi fora,
e direi come v'amai lungiamente
più ca Piramo Tisbia dolzemente,
ed ameragio infin ch'eo vivo ancora.

Pier della Vigna

Love

*Love, in whom I wish and hope, has
given me, my beauty, the reward of you.
I save myself, waiting for good weather
and season, until my hope becomes real:
as a man who is on the sea waits for
good weather to continue his voyage
and spreads his sails at the right time,
and that hope never deceives him; I do
the same, my Lady, to come to you.*

*If I could come to you now, my love,
like a thief at night and never be seen!
It would be such joyous luck for me,
if love were to do me so great a favor.
I would be so eloquent, love, and tell you
that I have loved you for so long, more
sweetly than Pyramus loved Thisbe,
and I will love you as long as I live.*

13

Vostro amor è che mi tene in disio,
e donami speranza con gran gioia,
ch'eo non curo s'io dollio od ò martiro
membrando l'ora ched io vegno a voi;
ca s'io troppo dimoro, aulente lena,
pare ch'io pera, e voi me perderete.
Adunque, bella, se ben mi volete,
guardate ch'eo no mora in vostra spera.

In vostra spera vivo, donna mia,
e lo mio core adesso a voi dimando,
e l'ora tardi mi pare che sia
che fino amore a vostro cor mi manda;
e guardo tempo che mi sia a piaciere
e spanda le mie vele inver voi, rosa,
a prendo porto là 've si riposa
lo meo core al vostro insegnamento.

My love of you makes me desire,
and gives me hope and great joy,
for I do not care if I suffer or have
sorrow if I can think of the moment
when I shall come to you; if I delay
too long, my fragrant love, it seems
I would die and that you will lose me.
So, my beauty, if you love me, watch
over me lest I die hoping for you.

I live hoping for you, my lady, and
now I ask my heart back from you,
and it seems late for love to bring me
to your heart; and I watch for the time
that you will favor my hope, when I may
spread my sails towards you, my rose,
and rest my heart in your secure harbor.

Richard A. Branyon

Guido Guinizelli (c.1240-1276)

Vedut' ho la lucente stella diana

Vedut' ho la lucente stella diana,
ch'appare anzi che 'l giorno rend'albore,
c'ha preso forma di figura umana,
sovr'ogni'altra mi par che dea splendore;
viso di neve colorato in grana
occhi lucenti gai e pien d'amore;
non credo che ne mondo sia cristiana
sì piena di beltate e di valore.

Ed io da lo su' amor son assalito
con sì fera battaglia di sospiri
ch'avanti a lei di dir non seri'ardito:
così conoscessa'ella i miei disiri,
chè, senza dir, di lei seria servito
per la pietà ch'avrebbe de' martiri.

Guido Guinizelli

I Have Seen the Shining Star

I have seen the shining star of morning
which appears before dawn yields its first light,
and which has taken the form of a human being.
I think she gives more splendor than any other.
A face like snow, tinged with red, shining eyes
that are gay and full of love; I do not believe
there is a single girl in the whole world
so full of beauty and worth.

And I am on fire with a love so fierce
and utter sighs so violent that I do not
dare say a single word in her presence.
I wish that she only knew of my desires,
so that, without speaking, she should show
pity on me for the torments that I suffer.

Richard A. Branyon

Cecco Angiolieri (1260-1313)

Maledetto

Maledetto e distrutto sia da Dio
lo primo punto, ch'io innamorai
di quella, ed ogn'altro sollazzo ha in oblio;
e si fa tanto tormento esser mio,
che 'n corpo d'uom non ne fu tanto mai:
e non le pare ever fatto anco assai,
tant'è 'l su' cor giude', pessimo e rio.

E non pensa se non com'ella possa
far a me cosa, che mi scoppi 'l cuore:
di questa oppinion ma' non fu mossa.
E di lei non mi posso gittar fuore,
tant'ho la ment'abbarbagliat'e grossa,
c'ho men sentor, che non ha l'uom, che mòre.

Cecco Angiolieri

A Curse

May God curse and destroy the
first moment that I fell in love with
the one who takes such pleasure in
bringing me sorrow, and is oblivious
to all other happiness; and causes me
such torment, that never before was
there so much pain in the body of a man:
and she doesn't think that she has done
enough yet, so evil and pitiless her heart.

And she thinks of nothing else except how
she may do things to break my heart: she
has never gone beyond this single idea.
But I cannot escape her reach, my mind
is so bewitched and stupefied that I now
have less feeling in me than a dying man.

Richard A. Branyon

Guido Cavalcanti (1240-1300)

Sonetti 1

Voi, che per gli occhi mi passaste al core
E destaste la mente che dormia,
Guardate a l' angosciosa vita mia
Che sospirando la distrugge Amore.
E' vien tagliando di si gran valore
Ch' e' deboletti spiriti van via:
Riman figura sol' en segnoria
E voce alquanta che parla dolore.
Questa vertù d' amor che m' a disfacto,
Da' vostr' occhi gentil presta si mosse;
Un dardo mi gitto dentro dal fianco.
Si giunse ritto 'l colpo al primo tracto,
Che l' anima tremando si riscosse,
Veggendo morto 'l cor nel lato manco.

Guido Cavalcanti

Sonnet 1

You, who do breach mine eyes and touch the heart,
  And start the mind from her brief reveries,
  Might pluck my life and agony apart,
  Saw you how love assaileth her with sighs,
And lays about him with so brute a might
  That all my wounded senses turn to flight.
  There's a new face upon the seigniory,
  And new is the voice that maketh loud my grief.
Love, who hath drawn me down through devious ways,
  Hath from you noble eyes so swiftly come!
  'Tis he who hath hurled the dart, wherefrom my pain,
First shot's resultant! and in flanked amaze
  See how my affrighted soul recoileth from
  That sinister side wherein the heart lies slain.

Ezra Pound

Guido Cavalcanti

Ballata 5

Veggio ne gli occhi de la donna mia
  Un lume pien di spiriti d'Amore,
  Che portano un piacer novo nel core,
  Si che vi desta d'allegrezza vita.

Cosa m'avvien, quand'io le son presente,
  Ch'i' non la posso a lo 'ntelletto dire:
  Veder mi par de le sue labbia uscire
  Una sì bella donna, che la mente
  Comprender non la può che 'mmantenente
  Ne nasce un altra di bellezza nova:
  Da la qual par, ch'una stella si mova,
  E dica: Tua salute è dipartita.

Là dove questa bella donna appare
  S'ode una voce, che le vien davanti,
  E par, che d'umiltà 'l suo nome canti
  Sì dolcemente, che s'io 'l vo' contare,
  Sento che'l suo valor mi fa tremare;
  E movonsi ne l'anima sospiri,
  Che dicon: Guarda, se tu costei miri,
  Vedrai la sua virtù nel ciel salita.

Guido Cavalcanti

Ballata 5

Light do I see within my Lady's eyes
And loving spirits in its plenisphere
Which bear in strange delight on my heart's care
Till Joy's awakened from that sepulchre.

That which befalls me in my Lady's presence
Bars explanation intellectual,
I seem to see a lady wonderful
Spring forth between her lips, one whom no sense
Can fully tell the mind of, and one whence
Another, in beauty, springeth marvelous,
From whom a star goes forth and speaketh thus:
"Now thy salvation is gone forth from thee."

There where this Lady's loveliness appeareth,
Is heard a voice which goes before her ways
And seems to sing her name with such sweet praise
That my mouth fears to speak what name she beareth,
And my heart trembles for the grace she weareth,
While far in my soul's deep the sighs astir
Speak thus: "Look well! For if thou look on her,
Then shalt thou see her virtue risen in heaven."

> *Ezra Pound*

Dante Alighieri (1265-1321)

La vita nuova: Canzone 1 (1–14)

Donne ch' avete intelletto d' amore,
  I' vo' con voi de la mia donna dire,
  Non perch' io creda sua laude finire,
  Ma ragionar per isfogar la mente.
  Io dico che pensando il suo valore,
  Amor sì dolce mi si fa sentire,
  Che s' io allora non perdessi ardire,
  Farei parlando innamorar la gente.
  E io non vo' parlar sì altamante,
  Ch' io divenisse per temenza vile.
  Ma tratterò del suo stato gentile
  A respetto di lei leggeramente,
  Donne e donselle amorose, con vui,
  Che non è cosa da parlarne altrui.

Dante Alighieri

The New Life: Canzone 1 (1-14)

Ladies that have an intelligence in love,
Of mine own lady I would speak with you;
Not that I hope to count her praises through,
But telling what I may, to ease my mind.
And I declare that when I speak thereof
Love sheds such perfect sweetness over me
That if courage failed not, certainly
To him my listeners must all be resigned.
Wherefore I will not speak in such large kind
That mine own speech should foil me, which were base;
But only will discourse of her high grace
In these poor words, the best that I can find,
With you alone, dear dames and damsels;
'Twere ill to speak thereof with any else.

D.G Rossetti

Dante Alighieri

La Commedia: Canto V

Quando risposi cominciai: "Oh lasso,
  Quanti dolci pensier, quanto disio
  Menò costoro al doloroso passo!"
Poi mi rivolsi a loro e parlai io,
  E cominciai: "Francesca, i tuoi martiri
  A lacrimar mi fanno tristo e pio.
Ma dimmi: all tempo de' dolci sospiri,
  A che e come concedette amore
  Che conosceste i dubbiosi disiri?"
E quella a me: "Nessun maggior dolore
  Che ricordarsi del tempo felice
  Nella miseria; e ciò sa il tuo dottore.
Ma s'a conoscer la prima radice
  Del nostro amor tu hai contanto affetto
  Dirò come colui che piange e dice.

Dante Alighieri

The Divine Comedy: Canto 5

When I replied, my words began: "Alas,
 how many gentle thoughts, how deep a longing,
 had led them to this agonizing pass!"
Then I addressed my speech again to them,
 and I began: "Francesca, your affliction
 moves me to tears of sorrow and of pity.
But tell me, in the time of gentle sighs,
 with what and in what way did Love allow you
 to recognize your still uncertain longings?"
And she to me: "There is no greater sorrow
 than thinking back upon a happy time
 in misery, and this your teacher knows.
Yet if you long so much to understand
 the first root of our love, then I shall tell
 my tale to you as one who weeps and speaks.

Noi leggevamo un giorno per diletto
  Di Lancialotto come amor lo strinse:
  Soli eravamo e senza alcun sospetto.
Per più fiate li occhi ci sospinse
  Quella lettura, e scolorocci il viso;
  Ma solo un punto fu quel che ci vinse.
Quando leggemmo il disiato riso
  Esser baciato da cotanto amante
  Questi, che mai da me non fia diviso,
La bocca mi baciò tutto tremante.
  Galeotto fu il libro e chi lo scrisse:
  Quel giorno più non vi leggemmo avante."
Mentre che l'uno spirito questo disse,
  L'altro piangea, sì che di pietate
  Io venni men, così com'io morisse;
E caddi come corpo morto cade.

One day, to pass the time away, we read
  of Lancelot, how love had overcome him.
  We were alone, and we suspected nothing.
And time and time again that reading led
  our eyes to meet, and made our faces pale,
  and yet one point alone defeated us.
When we had read how the desired smile
  was kissed by one who was so true a lover,
  this one, who never shall be parted from me,
While all his body trembled, kissed my mouth.
  A Gallehault indeed, that book and he
  who wrote it, too; that day we read no more."
And while one spirit said these words of pity to me,
  the other wept, so that, because of pity,
  I fainted, as if I had met my death.
And then I fell as a dead body falls.

  Allen Mandelbaum

Dante Alighieri

Il convivio: Sestina 1 (7–39)

Similemente questa nuova donna
  Si sta gelata, come neve all' ombra,
  Che non la muove, se non come pietra,
  Il dolce tempo, che riscalda i colli,
  E che gli fa tornar di bianco in verde,
  Perchè gli copre di fioretti e d' erba.

Quand' ella ha in testa una ghirlanda d' erba
  Trae della mente nostra ogni altra donna;
  Perchè si mischia il crespo giallo e 'l verde
  Sì bel, ch'Amor vi viene a stare all' ombra:
  Che m' ha serrato tra piccoli colli
  Più forte assai che la calcina pietra.

Le sue lellezze han più virtù che pietra,
  E 'l colpo suo non può sanar per erba;
  Ch' io son fuggito per piani e per colli,
  Per potere scampar da cotal donna;
  Ed al suo viso non mi può far ombra
  Poggio, nè muro mai, nè fronda verde.

Dante Alighieri

The Banquet: Sestina 1 (7–39)

Utterly frozen is this youthful lady,
Even as the snow that lies within the shade;
For she is no more moved than is the stone
By the sweet season which makes warm the hills
And alters them afresh from white to green
Covering their sides again with flowers and grass.

When on her hair she sets a crown of grass
The thought has no more room for to her lady,
Because she weaves the yellow with the green
So well that Love sits down there in the shade,—
Love who has shut me in among low hills
Faster than between walls of granite-stone.

She is more bright than is a precious stone;
The wound she gives may not be healed with grass:
I therefore had fled far over plains and hills
For refuge from so dangerous a lady;
But from her sunshine nothing can give shade,—
Not any hill, no wall, nor summer-green.

Io l' ho veduta già vestita a verde
  Sì fatta, ch' ella avrebbe messo in pietra
  L'Amor ch' io porto pure alla sua ombra:
  Ond' io l' ho chiesta in un bel prato d' erba
  Innamorata, com' anco fu donna,
  E chiuso intorno d' altissimi colli.

Ma ben ritorneranno i fiumi a' colli
  Prima che questo legno molle e verde
  S' infiammi (come suol far bella donna)
  Di me, che mi torrei dormir su pietra
  Tutto il mio tempo, e gir pascendo l' erba,
  Sol per vedere de' suoi panni l' ombra.

Quandunque i colli fanno più nera ombra,
  Sotto il bel verde la giovane donna
  Gli fa sparir, come pietra sott' erba.

A while ago, I saw here dressed in green,—
So fair, she might have wakened in a stone
This love which I do feel even for her shade;
And therefore, as one woos a graceful lady,
I wooed her in a field that was all grass
Girdled about with very lofty hills.

Yet shall the streams turn back and climb the hills
Before Love's flame in the damp wood and green
Burn, as it burns within a youthful lady,
For my sake, who would sleep away in stone
My life, or feed like beasts upon the grass,
Only to see her garments cast a shade.

How dark so ever the hills throw out their shade,
Under her summer-green the beautiful lady
Covers it, like a stone covered in grass.

      D.G. Rossetti

Cino da Pistoia (1270-1337)

Sonetto per Selvaggia

Come non è con voi a questa festa,
  Donne gentili, lo bel viso adorno?
  Perchè non fu da voi staman richiesta
  Che ad onorar venisse questo giorno?
Vedete ogn'uomo, che si mette in chiesta
  Per vederla, girandosi d'intorno;
  E guardan qua, u' per lo più s'arresta;
  Poi miran me, che sospirar non storno.
Oggi aspettavo veder la mia gioia
  Stare tra voi, e veder lo cor mio,
  Che a lei, come a sua vita, s'appoia.
Or io vi prego, donne, sol per Dio,
  Se non volete ch'io di cio mi moia,
  Fate sì che stasera la vegg'io.

Cino da Pistoia

Sonnet for Selvaggia

Why is she not with you upon this feast,
  Fair ladies, she whose lovely face I praise?
  Why did you not this morning make request
  That she should honor this, my day of days?
You see each man who puts himself in quest
  To see her, turning round within a maze;
  They look for her, where she is wont to rest;
  Then look at me, who stand and sigh and gaze.
Today I hoped to look on my delight
  Standing among you, and to see my heart,
  Which clings to her, as for its life and might.
Now do I beg you, ladies, in good part,
  If you should wish to save me from death's sight,
  Bring it about that I see her tonight.

  L.R. Lind

Francesco Petrarca (1304-1374)

Pace non trovo, e non ho da far guerra

Pace non trovo, e non ho da far guerra;
  E temo, e spero; et ardo, e son un ghiaccio;
  E volo sopra 'l cielo, e giaccio in terra;
  E nulla stringo, e tutto 'l mondo abbraccio.
Tal m'ha in pregion, che non m' apre nè serra,
  Nè per suo mi riten nè scioglie il laccio;
  E non m' ancide Amore, e non mi sferra,
  Nè mi vuol vivo nè mi trae d' impaccio.
Veggio senza occhi, e non ho lingua, e grido;
  E bramo di perir, e cheggio aita;
  Et ho in odio me stesso, et amo altrui.
Pascomi de dolor, piangendo rido;
  Egualmente mi spiace morte e vita:
  In questo stato son, donna, per vui.

Francesco Petrarca

I Find No Peace and Bear No Arms

I find no peace and bear no arms for war,
  I fear, I hope: I burn yet shake with chill;
  I fly the Heavens, huddle to earth's floor,
  Embrace the world yet all I grasp is nil.
Love will not close nor shut my prison's door
  Nor claim me his nor leave me to my will;
  He slays me not yet holds me evermore;
  Would have me lifeless yet bound to my will.
Eyeless I see and tongueless I protest,
  And long to perish while I succor seek;
  Myself I hate and would another woo.
I feed on grief, I laugh with sob-racked breast,
  And death and life alike to me are bleak:
  My lady, thus I am because of you.

        T.G. Bergin

Francesco Petrarca

Mille fiate, o dolce mia guerrera

Mille fiate, o dolce mia guerrera,
  Per aver co' begli occhi vostri pace
  V'aggio proferto il cor, m'a voi non piace
  Mirar sì basso colla mente altera;

E, se di lui fors' altra donna spera,
  Vive in speranza debile e fallace:
  Mio, perchè sdegno ciò ch'a voi dispiace,
  Esser non può già mai così com' era.

Or s' io lo scaccio, et e' non trova in voi
  Ne l'esilio infelice alcun soccorso,
  Né sa star sol, né gire ov'altri il chiama,

Poria smarrire il suo natural corso:
  Che grave colpa fia d'ambeduo noi,
  E tanto più de voi, quanto più v'ama.

Francesco Petrarca

A Thousand Times My Sweet Warrior

A thousand times my sweet warrior,
  To make peace with your beautiful eyes,
  I've offered you my heart; but you like not
  To gaze so low with your mind so proud:
And, if for him perhaps some other lady
  Hopes, she lives in hope that is weak and false:
  Mine, because I scorn what displeases you,
  Can never be such as it once was.
Now, if I chase him out and he finds not
  In unhappy exile some help from you,
  Neither apt to stay alone nor go where
Others call, he could lose life's natural course:
  Which would be to both of us a grave blow;
  And much more for you, by how much he loves.

    Jack D'Amico

Francesco Petrarca

Or ch 'l ciel e la terra e 'l vento tace

Or che 'l ciel e la terra e 'l vento tace
  E le fere e gli augelli il sonno affrena,
  Notte il carro stellato in giro mena,
  E nel suo letto il mar senz' onda giace,
Vegghio, penso, ardo, piango; e chi mi sface
  Sempre m' è inanzi per mia dolce pena:
  Guerra è 'l mio stato, d'ira e di duol piena;
  E sol di lei pensando ho qualche pace.
Così sol d'una chiara fonte viva
  Move 'l dolce e l' amaro, ond' io mi pasco;
  Una man sola mi risana e punge.
E perchè 'l mio martir non giunga a riva
  Mille volte il dì moro e mille nasco;
  Tanto de la salute mia son lunge.

Francesco Petrarca

The Wind and Earth and Heavens Rest

Now while the wind and earth and heavens rest,
  While sleep holds beast and feathered bird in fee
  And high above a calm and aweless sea
  The silent stars obey the night's behest,
Lie awake and yearning, sore distressed
  And racked by thoughts of my sweet enemy,
  Yet though her face recalled brings death to me
  'Tis only with such dreams I soothe my breast.
So from one living fountain, gushing clear,
  Pour forth alike the bitter and the sweet,
  And one same hand can deal me good or ill.
Whence every day I die anew of fear
  And live again to find that hope's a cheat,
  And peace of heart and mind escapes me still.

        T.G. Bergin

Giovanni Boccaccio (1313-1375)

Decameron: giornata II

Amor, s'io posso uscir de' tuoi artilgli,
aooena creder posso
che alcuno altro uncin mai più mi pigli.

Io entrai giovanetta en la tua guerra,
quella credendo somma e dolce pace,
e ciascuna mia si fida face;
ti; disleal tiranno aspro e rapace,
tosto mi fosti addosso
con le tue armi e co' crudel roncigli.

Poi, circondata dalle tue catene,
a quel che nacque per la morte mia,
piena d'amare lagrime e di pene
presa mi desti, ed hammi in sua belìa;
ed è sì cruda la sua signoria,
che già mai non l'ha mosso
sospir nè pianto alcun che m'assottigli.

Giovanni Boccaccio

The Decameron, Day 2

*Love, if I can get free from your claws, I can
hardly imagine any other hook will ever take me.*

*I entered into your war when I was young, thinking
it would be the sweetest and highest peace, laying
my arms on the ground, as confidently as
one who trusts; vicious, deceitful, dishonorable
tyrant, you who seized me immediately
with your arms and cruel claws.*

*Then, tangled in your chains you held me captive,
full of tears and grief, to him who was born for my
death, and he has me in his thrall, and he is such
a cruel master and he has never been moved,
not even once, by my sighing and weeping.*

Li prieghi miei tutti glien porta il vento:
nullo n'ascolta nè ne vuole udire;
per che ognora cresce il mio tormento,
onde 'l viver m'è noi' nè noi' nè so morire;
deh! dolgati, signor, del mio languire;
fa' tu quel ch'io non posso:
dalmi legato dentro a' tuoi vincigli.

Se questo far non vuogli, almeno sciogli
i legamai annodati da speranza;
deh! io ti priego, signor, che tu vogli:
chè, se tu 'l fai, ancor porto fidanza
di tornar bella qual fu mia usanza,
ed il dolor rimosso,
di bianchi fiori ornarmi e di vermigli.

*The wind hears all my prayers to him; he will
not listen to me or consider my pleas; thus my
anguish increases each day, so that living is
tedious, but yet I cannot die; O grieve master,
for my sake, bring about what I cannot do;
deliver him to me in your bonds.*

*If you will not do this, at least release me
from the ties bound by hope, I beg you,
master, please; because if you do, I feel
sure I shall become beautiful again, as I
used to be, and when sorrow has been
lifted from me I shall dress myself with
white and crimson flowers.*

Richard A. Branyon

Matteo Maria Boiardo (1441-1494)

Ligiadro veroncello

Ligiadro veroncello, ove è colei
  Che di sua luce aluminar te sòle?
  Ben vedo che il tuo danno a te non dole;
  Ma quanto meco lamentar te dèi!
Chè, senza sua vaghezza, nulla sei;
  Deserti i fiori e secche le viole:
  Al veder nostro il giorno non ha sole,
  La notte non ha stelle senza lei.
Pur mi rimembra che te vidi adorno,
  Tra' bianchi marmi e il colorito fiore,
  De una fiorita e candida persona.
A' tuoi balconi allor se stava Amore,
  Che or te soletto e misero abbandona,
  Perchè a quella gentil dimora intorno.

Matteo Maria Boiardo

Graceful Balcony

O graceful balcony, where is she that
with her gleam was wont to lighten thee?
Well do I perceive thy loss not grieves thee,
and yet thou shouldst lament with me,
For lacking all her beauty, thou are naught!
Drooping the flowers and dry the violets!
Lacking her, day has no sun,
the night has no stars for me.
Yet I remember that I saw thee decked,
among white marbles and colored flowers,
with one both white and flower-like.
Love stood then upon thy terraces but
now abandons thee to grief and solitude
because he dwells beside that gentle one.

Richard Aldington

Lorenzo de' Medici (1449-1492)

Vidi madonna sopra un fresco rio

Vidi madonna sopra un fresco rio
  Tra verdi frondi e liete donne starsi;
  Tal che dalla prima ora in qua ch' io arsi
  Mai vidi il viso suo più bello e pio.
Questo contentò in parte il mio desio,
  E all'alma diè cagion di consolarsi;
  Ma poi partendo il cor vidi restarsi,
  Crebbon vie più i pensier e 'l dolor mio.
Chè già il sole inchinava all' occidente,
  E lasciva la terra ombrosa e oscura;
  Onde il mio sol s'ascose in altra parte.
Fe il primo ben più trista assai la mente.
  Ah quanto poco al mondo ogni ben dura!
  Ma il rimembrar si tosto non si parte.

Lorenzo de' Medici

I Saw My Lady by a Cool, Fresh Stream

I saw my lady by a cool, fresh stream
  Among green branches and gay ladies stand;
  Since the first hour when I felt love's hot brand
  I never saw her face more lovely gleam.
This sight fulfilled in part my fondest dream
  And over my soul put reason in command;
  But when I left, my heart stayed at her hand,
  My fears and grief the greater came to seem.
When now the sun bent downwards to the west,
  And left the earth in shadow and in night,
  Then my own sun was hidden from its ray.
The setting sun more sadness brought at best.
  How all too little lasts this world's best light!
  But memory does not so soon fade away.

  L.R. Lind

Angelo Poliziano (1454-1494)

Io ti ringrazio, Amore

Io ti ringrazio, Amore,
d'ogni pena e tormento,
e son contento, omai d'ogni dolore.

Contento son di quanto ho mai sofferto,
Signor, nel tuo bel regno;
poi che per tua merzè sanza mio merto
m'hai dato un sì gran pegno,
poi che m'hai fatto degno
d'un sì beato riso,
che 'n paradiso, n'ha portato il core.
Io ti ringrazio, Amore.

In paradiso el cor n'hanno portato
que'begli occhi ridenti,
ov'io ti vidi, Amore, star celato
con le tue fiamme ardenti.
O vaghi occhi lucenti
che 'l cor tolto m'avete,
onde traete, sì dolce valore?
Io ti ringrazio, Amore.

Angelo Poliziano

I Thank You, Love

I thank you, Love,
for every pain and torment,
and I am happy now for every sorrow.

I am happy for what I have suffered,
Master, in your marvelous kingdom; since
in your kindness, so undeserving, you have
given me such a promise, since you have
made me worthy of such a blessed smile
that has carried my heart to paradise.
I thank you, Love.

Those lovely eyes have carried my heart
to paradise, where I saw you, Love, hidden
in your growing flames. O shining eyes
that have taken my heart, where do
you obtain such sweet power?
I thank you, Love.

I' ero già della mia vita in forse:
madonna in bianca vesta
con un riso amoroso mi soccorse,
lieta bella et onesta:
dipunta avea la testa
di rose e di viole,
gli occhi che 'l sole, avanzan di splendore.
Io ti ringrazio, Amore.

*I doubted for my life; but my lady
dressed in white saved me with a loving
smile, happy, beautiful and modest. Her
hair was decked with roses and violets,
her eyes surpassed the sun in brightness.
I thank you, Love.*

   Richard A. Branyon

Ludovico Ariosto (1474-1533)

Orlando Furioso: Capitulo VIII

O più che 'l giorno a me lucida e chiara,
 dolce, gioconda, aventurosa notte,
quanto men ti sperai tanto più cara.
Stelle a furti d'amor soccorrer dotte,
che minuisti il lume, nè per vui
mi fur l'amiche tenebre interrotte.

Sonno propizio, che lasciando dui
vigili amanti soli, così oppresso
avevi ogn'altro, che invisibil fui.
Benigna porta, che con sì sommesso
e con sì basso suon mi fusti aperta,
ch'a pena ti senti chi t'era presso.

O mente ancor di non sognar incerta,
quando abbracciar da la mia dea mi vidi,
e fu la mia con la sua bocca inserta.
O benedetta man, ch'indi mi guidi;
o cheti passi che m'andate inanti;
o camera, che poi così m'affidi.

Ludovico Ariosto

Orlando Furioso, Chapter 8

O night, more clear and shining, sweeter,
happier and more fortunate than day, so
much dearer that I hardly expected you.
Stars that attempt to hide love's thefts
that have dimmed your lights, not by you
were the friendly shadows broken.

Timely sleep, that leaving two lovers
alone, had overcome everyone else,
that I was almost invisible.
Kind door, that was opened with
a muffled sound so soft that he who
was close by hardly heard a sound.

O mind, uncertain if it dreamed or not,
when I saw myself held by my goddess
and my mouth was enclosed in hers.
O blessed hand, that leads me next,
O quiet steps that go before me.
O room that locked me in secure.

O complessi iterati, che con tanti
nodi cingete i fianchi, il petto, il collo,
che non ne fan più l'edere o li acanti.
Bocca ove ambrosia libo nè satollo
mai ne ritorno; o dolce lingua, o umore,
per cui l'arso mio cor bagno e rimollo.

Fiato, che spiri assai più grato odore
che non porta de l'indi o da sabei
fenice al rogo, in che s'incende e more.
O letto, testimon de' piacer miei;
letto cagion ch'una dolcezza io gusti,
che non invideo il lor nettare ai dèi.
O letto donator de' premi giusti,
letto, che spesso in l'amoroso assalto
mosso, distratto ed agitato fusti.
Voi tutti ad un ad un, ch'ebbi de l'alto
piacer ministeri, avrò in memoria eterna,
e quanto è il mor poter, sempre vi esalto.

O repeated embraces, that bind hips,
breast, neck with so many twines that
the ivy or acanthus have no more.
Mouth, from which I sup ambrosia,
not ever satiated, O soft tongue, O dew,
in which I bathe and soften my burnt heart.

Breath, which inhales far more pleasant
fragrances than the phoenix on his pyre
on which he flames and dies.
O bed, witness to my pleasures;
bed, cause of my tasting a sweetness
that I do not envy the gods their nectar.
All of you, one by one, shall I keep in my
everlasting eternal memory as ministers of
pleasure and I praise you with all my power.

George R. Kay

Michelangelo Buonarroti (1475-1564)

Madrigale 178

A l'alto tuo lucente diadema
Per la strada erta e lunga
Non è, Donna, chi giunga,
S'umilità non v'aggiugni e cortesia:
Il montar cresce, e 'l mio valore scema,
E la lena mi manca e mezza via.
Che tua beltà pur sia
Superna, al cor par che diletto renda,
Che d'ogni rara altezza è ghiotto e vago:
Po' per gioir della tua leggiadria,
Bramo pur che discenda
Là dov'aggiungo. E 'n tal pensier m'appago,
Se 'l tuo sdegno presago,
Per basso amare e alto odiar tuo stato,
A te stessa perdona 'l mio peccato.

Michelangelo Buonarroti

Madrigal 178

Lady, up to your high and shining crown
By the long, narrow route
None can attain without
Your adding your humility and grace.
The climbing stiffens and my strength runs down,
And by the halfway point I am out of breath.
It seems the ranking place
Your beauty holds can make my heart content,
Which yearns greedily for all special height;
And yet, to revel in your loveliness
I long for your descent
Where I can reach, being reassured in thought
That your foreseeing slight
Toward me who hates your high state, loves the lower,
May grant yourself forgiveness for my error.

Creighton Gilbert

Gaspara Stampa (1523-1554)

Per le saette tue, Amor

Per le saette tue, Amor, ti giuro,
e per la tua possente e sacra face,
che, se ben questa m'arde e 'l cor mi sface,
e quelle mi feriscon, non mi curo;
quantunque nel passato e nel futuro
qual l'une acute, e qual l'altra vivace,
donne amorose, e prendi qual ti piace,
che sentisser giamai nè fian, nè furo;

perchè nasce virtù da questa pena
che'l senso del dolor vince ed abbaglia,
sì che on non duole, o non si sente appena.
Quel, che l'anima e 'l corpo mi travaglia,
è la temenza ch'a morir mi mena,
che 'l foco mio non sia foco di paglia.

Gaspara Stampa

The Arrows of Love

*By your arrows, Love, I swear, and by
your mighty sacred torch that, although
one burns me and wastes my years and
the others wound me, I do not mind;
however far you go into the past or into
the future, there never was, nor will be,
a loving woman, and take whomever
you wish, to feel the first as sharp and
the second as devouring as I do;*

*for a virtue is born from this pain of mine
that overcomes and stupefies the sense
of suffering, so that it no longer hurts, or
is hardly felt. That, and it tortures my
soul and body, is the fear which leads
me towards death, least my fire should
be merely a small blaze of straw.*

Richard A. Branyon

Torquato Tasso *(1544-1595)*

Io v'amo sol perchè

Io v'amo sol perchè voi siete bella,
e perchè vuol mia stella,
non ch'io speri da voi, dolce mio bene,
altro che pene.

E se talor gli occhi miei mostrate
aver qualche pietate,
io non spero da voi del pianger tanto
altro che pianto.

Nè, perchè udite i miei sospiri ardenti
che per voi sprago a i venti,
altro spera da voi questo mio core
se non dolore.

Lasciate pur ch'io v'ami e ch'io vi miri
e che per voi sospiri,
chè pene pianto e doglia è sol mercede
de la mia fede.

Torquato Tasso

I Love You Because

I love you simply because you are fair,
and my stars desire it
not that I hope for anything from you,
my sweet life, except misery.

And if you decide to show pity
sometimes for my eyes,
I do not hope for anything but
weeping for so much sadness.

Nor, because you hear my burning sighs,
that for you I allow the winds to hear,
does this heart of mine hope for
anything from you but sorrow.

Let me still love you and look on you
and sigh for you, since
sadness, weeping and sorrow are
the only rewards I have for my love.

Richard A. Branyon

Ugo Foscolo *(1778-1827)*

Di sè stesso

Perchè taccia il rumor d'una catena,
di lagrime, di speme, e d'amor vivo,
e di silenzi; chè pietà mi affrena
se con lei parlo, o di lei penso o scrivo.
Tu sol mi ascolti, o solitario rivo,
ove ogni notte Amor seco mi mena,
qui affido il pianto e i miei danni descrivo,
qui tutta verso del dolor la piena.

E narro come i grandi occhi ridenti
arsero d'immortal raggio il mio core,
come la rosea bocca, e i rilucenti
odorati capelli, ed il candore
delle divine membra, e i cari accenti
m'insegnarono alfin pianger d'amore.

Ugo Foscolo

On Himself

So that the rattling of the chain may be silent,
I live on tears, on hope, on love and silence;
for tenderness restrains me, if I speak with her,
or think or write of her. You alone listen to
me, oh lonely stream, where every night Love
leads me in his company, here I confide my
tears and pour out my sufferings, and here
confide in you the fullness of my sorrow.

And tell how those laughing eyes burnt my
heart with an immortal ray, how her mouth,
so like a rose, and the shimmering fragrant
locks of her hair, and the whiteness of her arms,
and her sweet voice taught me to weep for love.

Richard A. Branyon

Giacomo Leopardi (1798-1837)

Il primo amore (1-30)

Tornami a mente il dì che la battaglia
D'amor sentii la prima volta, e dissi:
Oimè, se quest'è amor, com'ei travaglia!

Che gli occhi al suol tuttora intenti e fissi,
Io mirava colei ch'a questo core
Primiera il varco ed innocente aprissi.

Ahi come mal mi governasti, amore!
Perché seco dovea sì dolce affetto
Recar tanto desio, tanto dolore?

E non sereno, e non intero e schietto,
Anzi pien di travaglio e di lamento
Al cor mi discendea tanto diletto?

Dimmi, tenero core, or che spavento,
Che angoscia era la tua fra quel pensiero
Presso al qual t'era noia ogni contento?

Quel pensier che nel dì, che lusinghiero
Ti si offeriva nella notte, quando
Tutto queto parea nell'emisfero:

Giacomo Leopardi

First Love (1–30)

*I remember the first day when
I fought the battle of love, I said:
Alas, if this is love, I grieve!
My eyes downcast, staring,
I wondered how my innocent heart
ventured into this new realm.*

*Ah, how wrongly you ruled me, Love!
Why should sweet emotion
lead to such longing and such pain.
Torn apart, thwarted, and never calm,
filled with sorrows and despair,
still my heart drowned in delight.*

*Tell me of your anguish, loving heart,
your horror at such a thought
each happiness turns to weary anxiety.
All day long, that thought remained,
and at night, driven by desire,
when the world around seemed quiet*

Tu inquieto, e felice e miserando,
M'affaticavi in su le piume il fianco,
Ad ogni or fortemente palpitando.

E dove io tristo ed afannato e stanco
Gli occhi al sonno chiudea, come per febre
Rotto e deliro il sonno venia manco.

Oh come viva in mezzo alle tenebre
Sorgea la dolce imago, e gli occhi chiusi
La contemplavan sotto alle palpebre!

Oh come soavissimi diffusi
Moti per l'ossa mi serpeano, oh come
Mille nell'alma instabili, confusi...

You were restless, happy and miserable.
I tossed and turned, fatigued on my bed,
and never stopped trembling.
Sad and afraid and exhausted,
I closed my eyes:
feverish dreams kept me from sleep.

How clearly out of the dark
her tender image appeared; my eyes
sealed I saw her on my closed eyelids.
How subtle were these confused emotions
that wandered through my consciousness.

Richard A. Branyon

Ferdinando Russo (1866-1927)

Scetate

Si duorme a si nun duorme, bella mia,
sciente pe nu mumento chesta voce.
Chi te vo bene sta mmiez'a sta via
pe te cantá sta canzuncella doce.

Ma tu nun duorme e nun te sì scetata.
Sta fenestella nun se vò arapì!
È nu ricamo sta mandulinata!
Scetate, bella mia, nun cchiù durmì!

'Ncielo se so arrucchiate ciento stelle,
tutte pe' sta a sentì chesta canzone;
dicevano tra loro li cchiù belle:
se vede ca nce tene a' passione!

È passione ca nun passa mai!
Passa lo munno, essa nun passarrà!
Tu, certo, a chesto nun nce penzarrai,
ma tu sì nata pe m'affatturà!

Ferdinando Russo

Wake Up

Whether you're sleeping or not, my beauty,
listen for a moment to this voice.
The one who loves you is in the middle of this street
to sing you this sweet little song.

But you're not asleep and you haven't woken up,
This window doesn't want to open!
This mandolin serenade is a mere embroidery!
Wake up, my beauty, don't sleep anymore!

In the sky one hundred stars have gathered,
all to listen to this song;
the most beautiful said among themselves:
you can see that it is filled with passion!

It is a passion that never passes away!
While the world will come to an end, it will never cease!
You surely, don't realize it.
but you were born to bewitch me!

Hermann W. Haller

Vincenzo Cardarelli (1887-1960)

Adolescente (1-31)

Su te, vergine adolescente
sta come un'ombra sacra.
Nulla è più misterioso
e adorabile e proprio
della tua carne spogliata.
Ma ti recludi nell'attenta veste
e abiti lontano
con la tua grazia,
dove non sai chi ti raggiungerà.
Certo non io. Se ti veggo passare,
a tanta regale distanza
con la chioma scilolta
e tutta la persona astata,
la vertigine mi si porta via.
Sei l'imporosa e liscia creatura
cui preme, nel suo respiro
l'oscuro gaudio della carne che appena
sopporta la sua pienezza.

Vincenzo Cardarelli

The Adolescent (1-31)

Upon you, adolescent virgin,
a sacred shadow seems to rest.
Nothing is more mysterious
and adorable and unique
than your flesh disrobed.
But you seclude yourself in careful dress,
and with your gracefulness
live in some distant land,
unaware of who will reach you there.
Surely not I. If I behold you walking by,
at such a queenly distance,
with your locks unbound
and your body straight,
vertigo sweeps me away.
You are the impenetrably smooth creature
in whose breathing stirs
the dark bliss of flesh that scarcely
can withstand its plenitude.

Nel sangue, che ha diffusioni
di fiamma, sulla tua faccia,
il cosmo fa le sue risa
come nell'occhio nero della rondine.
La tua pupilla è bruciata
del sole che dentro vi sta.
La tua bocca è serrata.
Non sanno le mani tue bianche
il sudore umiliante dei contatti,
E penso come il tuo corpo,
difficoltoso e vago,
fa disperare l'amore
nel cuor dell'uomo!

In the blood which fans out wide
in flames upon your face,
the cosmos has its laughter
as in the black eye of a swallow.
Your pupil is seared
by the sun within it.
Your mouth is locked tight.
Those white hands of yours do not know
the shameful sweat of handled flesh.
And I think of how your body,
tortuous and eager,
causes love to despair
in the heart of man!

Carlo Golino

Camillo Sbarbaro (1888-1967)

Ore che sei venuta

Ore che sei venuta,
che con passo di danza sei entrata
nella mia vita
come folata una stanza chiusa—
a festeggiarti, bene tanto atteso,
le parole mi mancano e la voce
e tacerti vicino già mi basta.

Il piglìo così che assorda il bosco
al nascere dell'alba, ammutolisce
quando sull'orizzonte balza il sole.

Ma te la mia inquietudine cervaca
quando ragazzo
nella notte d'estate mi facevo
alla finestra come soffocata:
che non sapevo, m'affannava il cuore.
E tutte sono le parole
che, come l'acque all'orlo che trabocca,
alla bocca venivano da sole,
l'ore deserte, quando s'avanzavan
puerilmente le mie labbra d'uomo
da sé, per una voglia di baciare…

Camillo Sbarbaro

Now That You Have Come

Now that you have come,
dancing into
my life
a guest in a closed room——
to welcome you, love longed for so long,
I lack the words, the voice,
and I am happy just in silence by your side.

The chirping that deafens the woods
at dawn, stills
when the sun leaps to the horizon.

But my unrest sought you,
when, as a boy,
on summer nights I came
stifled to the window:
for I didn't know, and it worried my heart.
And yours are all the words
that came, like water brimming over,
unbidden to my lips,
the desert hours, when childishly
my adult lips rose
alone, longing for a kiss...

      Catherine O'Brien

Giuseppe Ungaretti (1888-1970)

Cori descrittivi di stati d'animo di Didone

Dileguandosi l'ombra,
In lontananza d'anni,
Quando non laceravano gli affani,

L'allora, odi, puerile
Petto ergersi bramato
E l'occhio tuo allarmato
Fuoco incauto svelare dell'Aprile
Da un'odorosa gota.

Scherno, spettro solerete
Che rendi il tempo inerte
E lungamente la sua furia nota:

Il cuore roso, sgombra!
Ma potrà, mute lotte
Sopite, dileguarsi da età, notte?

La sera si prolunga
Per un sospeso fuoco
E un fremito nell'erbe a poco a poco
Pare infinito a sorte ricongiunga.

Giuseppe Ungaretti

Choruses Descriptive of Dido's State of Mind

The disappearing shadow,
In a distance of years,
When sorrows did not wound,

You hear the youthful
Breast swell, desiring,
And your alarmed eye
Unveils the bold fire of April
From a perfumed cheek.

Scorn, an ubiquitous specter
Who makes time powerless
And its fury known at length,

Leave the broken heart!
But when the silent battles are over
Can night escape from eternity?

The evening is prolonged
By the suspended fire
And a shudder in the grass little by little
Appears to reunite the infinite with fate.

Lunare allora inavvertita nacque
Eco, e si fuse al brivido dell'acque.

Non so chi fu più vivo,
Il sussurrio sino all'ebbro rivo
O l'attenta che tenera si tacque.

Ora il vento s'è fatto silenzioso
E silenzioso il mare;
Tutto tace; ma grido
Il grido, sola, dela mio cuore,
Grido d'amore, grido di vergogna
Del mio cuore che brucia
Da quando ti mirai e m'hai guardata
E più non sono che un oggetto debole.

Then a surreptitious echo like the moon
Was born and fused with trembling water.

I do not know what was more alive,
The murmuring of the drunken stream
Or the silent expectant lover.

Now the wind has become silent.
Silent as the sea;
All is quiet; but I cry alone,
The cry of my heart,
Cry of love, cry of shame
Out of my heart that burns
Since I saw you and you looked at me
And I am nothing but a weak thing.

Richard A. Branyon

Albino Pierro (b. 1916)

Ti vògghie bbéne

«Ti vògghie bbéne quant'è granne u munne,»
mi dìcese cuntente e ié crére,
e ti vire nda ll'arie e si' na pinna
rusète supr'u fiète d'u vrascére.

Ti n'addònese, amore, ca nun chiange
nd'i vrazze tue e grire 'a cuntantizze?
Ié biniriche u iurne c'agghie nète,
si m'avit 'a nichè nda sti billizze.

Trèse nda ll'occhie tue com' 'a 'uce
d'u sóue mmenz'i frunne quann'è gghiurne,
e nun ci trove cchiù manche na cruce
e pure 'a notte è sempe menzeiurne.

Albino Pierro

I Love You

"My love for you is as big as the world,"
you tell me happily, and I believe you;
and I watch you in the air, a rosy
feather on the brazier's breath.

Do you notice, love, that I'm not crying
in your arms but shouting for gladness?
I bless the day that I was born,
that has drowned me now in so much beauty.

I enter into your eyes, like sunlight
in the leaves when it is day.
and there I find not one remaining cross
and even the night is always noon.

Pó, mèna a mène, aunìte ci traséme,
chi la sàpete addù, come nd'u cée,
'a vampa di nu foche e le sintéme
ca nd'u schème ci mòrete 'a cannée.

I'è stète troppe u scure troppe i chiove
ca s'ànne trapanète; mó' 'ucente
sempe at' 'a i'èsse ll'arie e nda stu core
noste na vocia ntutte ci àmm' 'a sente.

«Amore,» chiste è chille c'àt' 'a dice
sta vocia; mó' stu munne è tante belle.
Nun c'è nisciune cchiù ca i'è nfilice
e nun su' fridde cchiù nd'u cée i stelle.

Then, hand in hand, together we enter,
who knows just where or how, into heaven;
we see the blazing of a fire, and we can hear
the candle dying in the flame.

The dark has been too deep, too many the thorns
that pierced us through; now the air
will be forever radiant, and in our hearts
we'll hear only one single voice.

"Love" is what that voice will say;
the world has become so beautiful,
no one is unhappy anymore,
and the stars are no longer cold in the sky.

Hermann H. Haller

Italian Quotations and Proverbs

Di cor gentile è segno quando
fiamma un giovanetto incende.
Giraldi

Amor, s' io posso uscir de' tuoi artigli,
appeno reder posso che alcuno altro
uncin mai più mi pigli.
Boccaccio

Amor, che al cor gentil ratto s'apprende.
Dante

Amor, accesso di virtù, sempre altro accese,
pur che lo fiamma sua paresse fuore.
Dante

Amore la spinge e tira. Non
per elezion ma per destino.
Petrarca

It is a sign of a noble heart when a
young man burns with a flame of love.

Love, should I escape your snares, I doubt
that I can be trapped by any other means.

Love is quickly caught in the gentle heart.

Love, unkindled by virtue, always kindles
another love, providing its flame shines forth.

Love drives one not by choice but by fate.

Amore, e 'l cor gentil son un cosa.
Dante

Amor di nostra vita ultimo inganno.
Leopardi

Negli occhi porta la mia donna Amore,
per che si far gentil ciò ch' ella mira.
Dante

Chi più dir com' egli arde, è in picciol fusco.
Petrarca

Chi amo assai, soltante parlo poco.
Castiglione

Love and the gentle heart are the same things.

Love is the ultimate deception of our life.

In her eyes, my lady carries love and makes gentle everything that she looks upon.

To say how much you love is to love too little.

One who loves much often talks little.

Chi vive amante sai che delira, spesso si lagna
sempre suspira nè d'altro parla che di morir.
Metastasio

L'amore è un erba spontanea, non una pianta
da giardino.
Nievo

La foglia quando ama divena fiore, il fiore
quando ama diventa frutto.
Tagore

Lasciamo ai morti l'immortalià della gloria,
ma diamo ai vivi l'immortalità dell'amore.
Tagore

Il bene dell'uomo consiste nell'amore, come
quello della pianta deriva della luce.
Nievo

E son come d'amor baci baciati, gli
incontri di due cori amanti amati.
Guarini

*One who is in love acts delirious, he often
moans, always sighs, and speaks of death.*

*Love is a spontaneous grass, not a plant
which is carefully cultivated in the garden.*

*The leaf when loved becomes a flower,
the flower when loved becomes a fruit.*

*We leave to death the immortality of glory,
but we leave to life the immortality of love.*

*The existence of love derives from love,
as the plant derives life from the sun.*

*Kisses, when given in love, are the
joining together of two loving souls.*

L'amore nel cuore umano cresce e tramonta.
Guerrazzi

L'amore quanto più è bestia, tanto più sublime.
Copponi

*L'amore è dolcissima corrispondenza degli
spiriti, che di due anime ne compone una sola.*
Guerrazzi

*La beatitudine de essere amato raddolcisce
qualunque dolore.*
Foscolo

Triste è quella casa dove l'amor non ride.
Giacosa

Mé consiglio d'uomo sano Amor riceve.
Tasso

Love grows and wanes in the heart of man.

The more physical the love, the more sublime.

Love is the sweetest joining of spirits,
when two souls become as one.

The happiness of being in love
sweetens whatever pain exists.

Sad is the house where love does not live.

I would advise a sane man to receive love.

Amor ch'a nullo amato amar perdone.
Dante

Che dolce più che più giocondo stato
saria di quel d'un amoroso cuore.
Tasso

Che non più far d'un cuor i abbia suggetto,
avesto crudele, e traitor Amore.
Ariosto

Chi è ferito d'amoro strale d'altra piaga no teme.
Guarini

Chi ha l'amor ne petto, ha lo sprone al fianchi.
Giaccone

Chi fa all'amore è raro non sia costretto
a dire qualche bugia.
D'Annunzio

Love insists that love should be mutual.

*How sweet is the rapturous state of
soft passions in a heart full of love.*

*What he cannot do with the heart, he casts
out; how cruel the wicked ways of Love.*

*He who has been smitten by the arrows of love
is no longer afraid of any other wound.*

One with love in his breast has spurs in his side.

He who is in love is often compelled to deceive.

L'amore è la moneta coinata dalla banca di Dio.
Giaccone

L'affetto vero è un gran tesoro, è il più
grande che esista.
D'Azeglio

Al cor gentil ripara sempre Amore
come a le selva augello in la verdura.
Guinizelli

Gioia promette e manda pianto Amore.
Foscolo

Amor non lega troppo eguali tempre.
Gozzano

Il vero amore è una quite accesa.
Ungaretti

Love is the currency minted in God's bank.

*True love is a grand treasure; it is
the greatest treasure that exists.*

*A gentle heart always returns love
as a tall tree gives shade to the grass.*

The joy of love promotes and sustains it.

Love does not temper with equal force.

True love is a quiet, shining light.

Quanto è breve il sentiero, che dal finto
in amor conduce al vero.
Metastasio

L'amore certo l'amore, fuoco e fiamme
per un anno, cenere per trenta.
Lampedusa

Dovevamo saperlo che l'amore brucia la
vita e fa valore il tempo.
Cardarelli

Solo due prove certe ha l'amore; la noia
e la sconoscenza.
Tommaseo

D'amor ne regno non v'è contento,
che tel tormento no, sia minor.
Metastasio

Che felice amor fugge e non cura
tardo pentir, non libertà procurra.
Metastasio

How short is the path, an artificial
love is soon exposed by the truth.

Love, certainly love, fire and flames
for a year, then ashes for thirty years.

We must know that love is the flame
of life and makes time worthwhile.

There are only two things certain
about love: distress and ignorance.

Love is not content to merely reign, but
it must torment, nothing else satisfies.

One is happy to flee from love without care,
only to repent later and lose his freedom.

Le fanciulle pensano al matrimonio,
le maritate pensano all'amore.

Corona della vita, felicità senza pace, amore.

Amor nuovo va e viene, amor vecchio si mantiene.

L'amor è amaro, ma rinfranca il cuore.

Beltà e onesta vanno spesso in compagnia.

Amor non viva quando muor la speranza.

Young girls dream of marriage,
married women dream of love.

The crowning moment of our life, happiness
without peace, this is love.

New loves come and go, an old love remains.

Love is often bitter, but it reassures the heart.

Beauty and honesty are seldom seen together.

Love no longer lives when hope is dead.

L'amore è cieco, ma il matrimonio gli ridà la vista.

Amor senza baruffe, è amor che sa di muffa.

Non essere amati è solo sfortuna, non sapere amare è una tragedia.

Quando l'amore è in cocci non v'è mastice che la ricongiunga.

Quando l'amore vuol fuggire è inutile inseguirlo.

Chi vuol nascondere l'amore sempre lo manifesto.

Love is blind but marriage restores one's vision.

Love without strife is love that is smoldering.

Not to have been loved is a misfortune,
but not to have loved is a tragedy.

When love has fallen apart there is no
glue strong enough to hold it together.

When love flees it is futile to pursue it.

When one tries to hide love, one gives
the best evidence of its existence.

L'amore nella vita dell'uomo è una cosa
parte, ma nella donna è tutta la vita.

L'amore è una guida cieca, e quelli che le
seguano multo spesso si smarriscono.

Non è possibile nascondere l'amore ogli
occhi di chi ama.

La magia del primo amore consiste non
sapere ch' esse può sempre fini.

D'amor non s'intende che prudenza ad amore.

Il linguaggio dell'amore è negli occhi.

Love is only a portion of a man's life,
but it is the whole of a woman's life.

Love is a blind guide and those who follow
him often lose their way.

One cannot hide love from a lover's eyes.

The magic of the first love is the ignorance
that it can never end.

One who tries to unite prudence and love
knows nothing about love.

The language of love is in the eyes.

Il tempo di solito è bello quando si fa l'amore.

*E meglio certo, amare saggiamente, ma amare
scioccamente è meglio che no potere affatto amare.*

*Quando uno è innamorato comincia a ingannare
se stesso e foi finisce con l'ingannare gli altri.*

*L'amore nasce per la curiosità e perdura
per l'abitudine.*

*Tanto è possente amore quanto dai nostri
cor forza riceve.*

The weather is always fair when people are in love.

It is best to love wisely, no doubt, but to love foolishly is better than not to love at all.

When one is in love one begins to deceive oneself and ends by deceiving others.

Love is born by curiosity, endures by habit.

The power of love is determined by the strength the heart has given to it.

Nella sua prima passione la donna ama
l'amante, in tutte le altre non ama che l'amore.

L'amore della donna è scritto nell'acqua, la
fedeltà della donna è tracciata sulla sabbia.

Il vero paradiso non è già in cielo, è sulla
bocca della donna amata.

Il rumore d'un bacio non è così forte come quello del
cannone, ma la sua sco dura molti più lungo.

Per le donne v'è altro bene nella vita che l'amore.

In her first passion woman loves her lover,
in all others she is in love with love.

Declarations of a woman's love should be written
in water and her promises scribbled in the sand.

True paradise is not in the heavens but
upon the mouth of a woman in love.

The sound of a kiss is not as strong as that of a canon
but its echo may endure much longer.

For women, there is no good in life except love.

L'unico merito d'un uomo è il buon senso, ma il maggior valore di una donna è nella sua bellezza.

Il cielo non ha rabbia come l'amore diventato odio, nè l'inferno una furia come una donna disprezzata.

Una donna, la sua sorte è fatta dell'amore ch'ella acetta.

Colei che non ha mai amato, non ha mai vissuto.

I miei soli libri furono gli occhi delle donne e non m'isegnarno che pazzie.

Gli uomini hanno gli anni che sentono, e le donne quelli che mostrano.

The only merit of a man is his good sense, but the greatest merit of a woman is her beauty.

There is no rage in heaven like a love turned to hate and there is no fury in hell like a woman scorned.

A woman's fate is determined by the love she accepts.

A woman who has never loved has never lived.

My only books were the eyes of women and look what a fool I have become.

Men are as old as they feel, but women are as old as they look.

L'amor si nutrisce di mutuo sacrifizio.

Amor vero non diventa mai canuto.

Assenza nemico d'amore, quanto lontano
dall'occhi, tanto dal cuore.

Amor è il prezzo con cui si compra amor.

Chiusa fiamma è più ardente e se pur cresce.

Chi si marita in fretta, stenta adagio.

Love is nourished by mutual sacrifice.

True love can never become old.

*Absence is the enemy of love; one
who is out of sight is also out of heart.*

Love is the prize one buys with love.

A silent passion increases more ardently.

One who marries in haste repents at leisure.

Lungo è il cammino, ma l'amore è forte.

Amor, tosse, e fumo malamente si nascondano.

Chi ha la moglie bella sa che non è tutta sua.

Nella guerra d'amore vince chi fugge.

Senza Bacco e Cerere, Venere trema pel freddo.

Amante non sia chi coraggio non ha.

The road is long and difficult, but love conquers.

Love is a cough, and smoke cannot be hidden.

*One who has a beautiful wife knows that
he will have to share her with others.*

In the war of love, the one who flees wins.

Without wine and food, even Love grows pale.

One who wants to be a lover must be brave.

Amato non sarai, se à te solo penserai.

Amor dà per mercede gelosia e rotta fede.

Amor è cieco ma vede da lontano.

Amor e signoria non voglia compagnia.

Amore regge il suo regno senza spade.

Amor regge senza legge.

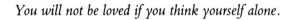

You will not be loved if you think yourself alone.

The result of love is jealously and broken faith.

Love is blind but can see far away.

Love and mastery are not companions.

Love rules his kingdom without a sword.

Love rules without any laws.

Quando la fame vien dentro la porte,
l'amore se ne va della finestra.

Gli amori nuovi fanno dimenticare i vecchi.

Amor fa molto, il denaro fa tutto.

Dov' è l'amore, là è l'occhio.
L'occhio attira l'amore.

Amor non conosce travaglio.

Sdegno cresce amore.

When poverty enters the door,
love goes out the window.

New love soon expels an old love.

Love does much; money does everything.

Where there is love, it is in the eyes.
Eyes reflect the passions of love.

Love perceives nothing as labor.

A quarrel is the renewing of love.

La carità ricopre ogni misfatto.

La gelosia è dura come l'inferno.

Non è amore senza gelosia.

Ogni disuguaglianza amor agguaglia.

L'amore è forte come la morte.

In premio d'amor, amor si rende.

Love conceals all of one's faults.

Jealousy can be as cruel as death.

Love is never without jealousy.

Love makes everything equal.

Love is as strong as death.

Love is the reward of love.

Il primo amore non si scorda mai.

La compiuta carità caccia fuori la paura.

Lontano degli occhi, lontano del cuore.

Fortuna al gioco, sfortuna in amore.

Amore non è senza amaro.

Sdegno d'amante poco dura.

Old loves are never forgotten.

Perfect love casts out all fears.

Far from sight, far from mind.

Lucky in cards, unlucky in love.

Love is never without troubles.

The anger of lovers lasts a short time.

Non si può dettar leggi al cuore.
Cosa per forza non vale scorza.

Per piacere amami poco se vuoi
amarmi a lungo.

Nessun amore più vero di quello che
muore non rivelato.

Non v'è nulla quaggiù più dolce dell'amore.

L'amore è cieco e gli innamorati non possono
vedere leggiadro follie che essi commettono.

Per dire la verità, la ragione e l'amore
se la fanno poco insieme.

One cannot make laws to rule the heart.
The power of love cannot be compelled.

Love me a little as long as you love me long.

There is no love so true as one which dies untold.

There is nothing in the world as sweet as love.

Love is blind and cannot see the pretty
follies which lovers themselves commit.

To tell the truth, love and reason are
seldom seen in the same company.